THE WORLD'S BIOMES

Wetlands

THE WORLD'S BIOMES

Deserts

Grasslands

Oceans

Rainforests

Wetlands

THE WORLD'S BIOMES

Wetlands

Kimberly Sidabras

MASON CREST
PHILADELPHIA

Mason Crest
450 Parkway Drive, Suite D
Broomall, PA 19008
www.masoncrest.com

© 2019 by Mason Crest, an imprint of National Highlights, Inc.

Printed and bound in the United States of America.

CPSIA Compliance Information: Batch #B2018.
For further information, contact Mason Crest at 1-866-MCP-Book.

First printing
1 3 5 7 9 8 6 4 2

Library of Congress Cataloging-in-Publication Data

Names: Sidabras, Kimberly, author.
Title: Wetlands / Kimberly Sidabras.
Description: Philadelphia : Mason Crest Publishers, [2018] | Series: The
   world's biomes | Audience: Age 12. | Audience: Grades 7 to 8. | Includes
   bibliographical references and index.
Identifiers: LCCN 2017047693 (print) | LCCN 2017050708 (ebook) | ISBN
   9781422277553 (ebook) | ISBN 9781422240403 (hardcover)
Subjects: LCSH: Wetland ecology—Juvenile literature. | Wetlands—Juvenile
   literature.
Classification: LCC QH541.5.M3 (ebook) | LCC QH541.5.M3 S4975 2018 (print) |
   DDC 577.68—dc23
LC record available at https://lccn.loc.gov/2017047693

THE WORLD'S BIOMES series ISBN: 978-1-4222-3794-6

QR CODES AND LINKS TO THIRD-PARTY CONTENT

Table of Contents

KEY ICONS TO LOOK FOR:

Words to understand: These words with their easy-to-understand definitions will increase the reader's understanding of the text while building vocabulary skills.

Sidebars: This boxed material within the main text allows readers to build knowledge, gain insights, explore possibilities, and broaden their perspectives by weaving together additional information to provide realistic and holistic perspectives.

Educational Videos: Readers can view videos by scanning our QR codes, providing them with additional educational content to supplement the text. Examples include news coverage, moments in history, speeches, iconic sports moments and much more!

Text-dependent questions: These questions send the reader back to the text for more careful attention to the evidence presented there.

Research projects: Readers are pointed toward areas of further inquiry connected to each chapter. Suggestions are provided for projects that encourage deeper research and analysis.

Series glossary of key terms: This back-of-the-book glossary contains terminology used throughout this series. Words found here increase the reader's ability to read and comprehend higher-level books and articles in this field.

 ## Words to Understand

acidic—containing acid.

delta—a fan-shaped region at a river's mouth.

estuary—the mouth of a river: the part that is tidal.

evaporation—the process by which a liquid becomes a gas.

fen—a peaty marsh that is low in acidity.

floodplain—a flat land flanking a river, which floods in the rainy season.

geological fault—a fracture in a bed of rocks.

mangrove—one of several types of tree that can grow in water.

migratory—making seasonal journeys between regions to breed or to escape an unsuitable climate.

peat—a spongy, wet soil made from rotted plant material.

sedge—a coarse kind of grass.

Swamp forest trees, such as these bald cypresses in Louisiana, often have trunks that are wide at their bases. This helps to stabilize them in the saturated soil where they grow.

What Are Wetlands?

A wetland is a region where water and land interact. It consists not only of the water and the land, but also of the plants that have adapted to live there. These plants contribute to the way the wetland develops.

There are many different types of wetland, ranging from swamps and *mangrove* forests in the tropics to *peat* bogs on windswept mountains. Large wetland areas such as the Florida Everglades in the United States, or the Okavango Delta in southern Africa, are famous for their rich and unique mixtures of wildlife.

Different Types of Wetland

Marshes are among the most common wetlands. They are usually shallow, and support beds of reeds and rushes. They get water directly from springs and rivers—especially when these waterways floods over their banks—as well as from rainfall. In river estuaries there are often areas of salt marsh that are flooded with every tide.

Swamps and swamp forests are regions where the soil is saturated with water, and usually flooded. Many exist around the edges of tropical lakes. Swamp forests are dominated by special types of trees that grow well in waterlogged soil.

Mangrove forests fringe the coasts of many tropical countries. They are tidal, so the trees that live there have to be able to grow with their roots in salt water. There are several different families of mangroves. Mangrove forests protect shorelines and support an immense variety of wildlife.

Sometimes dead plant material builds up in waterlogged areas quicker than it can decay. The resulting layer of slowly rotting plant material is known as peat. Peat bogs are wetlands where the peat has

Biome versus Ecosystem

A biome is a very large ecological area, with plants and animals that are adapted to the environmental conditions there. Biomes are usually defined by physical characteristics—such as climate, geology, or vegetation—rather than by the animals that live there. For example, deserts, rainforests, and grasslands are all examples of biomes. Plants and animals within the biome have all evolved special adaptations that make it possible for them to live in that area.

A biome is not quite the same as an ecosystem, although they function in a similar way. An ecosystem is formed by the interaction of living organisms within their environment. Many different ecosystems can be found within a single biome. Components of most ecosystems include water, air, sunlight, soil, plants, microorganisms, insects, and animals. Ecosystems exist on land and in water, with sizes ranging from a small puddle to an enormous swath of desert.

Large elephant herds flourish in Botswana's Okavango region. The area is rich in regularly flooded wetlands, where elephants can drink, bathe, and feed all year without having to migrate vast distances.

built up to a depth of at least 12 to 16 inches (30 to 40 cm). They are very *acidic*, and the soil does not have enough nutrients for most plants. *Fens*, on the other hand, are peatlands rich in nutrients and low in acidity.

Floodplains are lands beside rivers that are flooded regularly in the wet season. They can cover huge areas when the land is particularly flat. Floodplain soils are usually very rich in plant nutrients from the muddy silts deposited by the floodwaters.

Estuaries, *deltas*, and tidal flats are all regions where rivers enter the sea. They contain some of the planet's most complex wetlands, with regularly changing mixtures of fresh and salt water. An *estuary* is where a river widens as it joins the sea. A delta is an estuary that has silted up, so that the river fans out into many channels as it joins the sea. Between the channels and lagoons are reed-beds and expanses of tidal mud (tidal flats). The mud in an estuary is rich in nutrients because where fresh and salt water meet, chemicals and nutrient particles cling together and settle on the river bed.

Lakes often have wetland systems such as marshes and swamp forests around their shallows. Some lakes have constant inflows and outflows of water, while others have no outlets—they lose water only by *evaporation*. Lakes of this second type sometimes become "salt" lakes, because minerals in the lake ("salts") become more concentrated as the water evaporates.

The Planet's Major Wetland Areas

The Florida Everglades consist of grass and *sedge* marshlands, cypress swamps, and coastal mangroves. They are regularly flooded when Lake Okeechokee in the north overflows, but the flood area has been reduced in recent years to accommodate growing human communities. The Everglades once covered over 4,000 square miles (10,360 sq. km), but it is now about half that size. Some 2,360 square miles (6,109 sq. km) are managed by the National Park Service as Everglades National Park, the largest protected wilderness area east of the Rocky Mountains within the United States.

The South American Pantanal is one of the Earth's largest floodplains. It covers about 75,000 square miles (200,000 sq. km) of Brazil, Bolivia, and Paraguay, and is full of lakes, marsh-

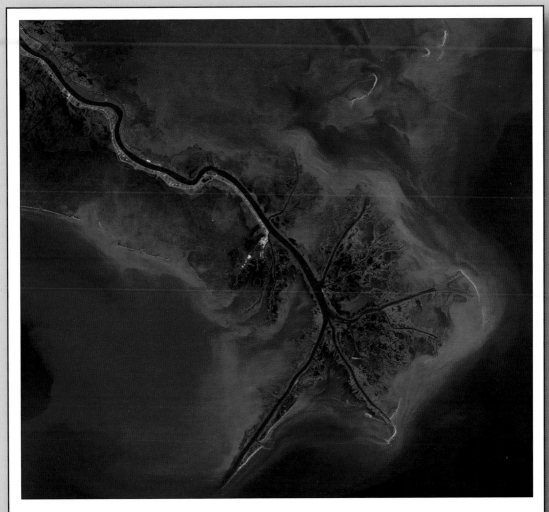

This satellite image of the Mississippi River Delta shows how a river's delta is made up of a large number of channels fanning out to meet the sea.

es, streams, and rivers. Floods cover much of the Pantanal in the rainy season, which lasts from December to March, but the floods sometimes continue until mid-June.

The Amazon Basin is a separate wetlands system that was created over millions of years by the Amazon River. It covers an area of up to 23,200 square miles (60,000 sq. km), and is a maze of floodplains and lakes. Seasonal floods cover many forest regions with water for months at a time. The enormous Amazon delta covers an area of 13,500 square miles (35,000 sq. km).

The Nine-Dragon River

Mekong means "Nine Dragons," and refers to the nine channels into which the river divides at its delta. The Mekong carries so much water following monsoons that it is higher than some of the smaller rivers feeding into it. Flood surges travel back up these tributary rivers, temporarily reversing their flow. In Cambodia this reverse flow moves up the Tonle Sap River, and swells the Great Lake upstream to five times its dry season area. After a pause, the flow returns to its normal direction, carrying with it large numbers of lake-breeding fish.

The Mekong River in Asia stretches 2,700 miles (4,350 km) from the highlands of Tibet to the South China Sea. Annual floods fertilize agricultural land in five different countries on the floodplains beside the river. However the construction of hydroelectric dams on the river has disrupted the natural flood cycles.

Educational Video

For an overview of the functions and importance of wetlands, scan here:

The Sunderbans in Bangladesh is the joint delta of the Ganges, Brahmaputra, and Meghna rivers. It contains the world's largest mangrove forest. The tides of the Bay of Bengal flood the streams and channels of the Sunderbans, and the area is probably the most important habitat for the royal Bengal tiger. The Sunderbans area is about one-third the size it was 200 years ago. Today, the swamps and river area covers 2,350 square miles (6,100 sq. km).

The Sudd is a huge swamp region in the country of South Sudan. The Sudd swamps are fed by the White Nile River, and form one of Africa's largest floodplains. Many *migratory* birds and mammals depend on the Sudd as a place to stop off and find food, while local cattle herders depend on its seasonal grasses.

The Okavango in northern Botswana is the world's largest inland delta, where the Okavango River spreads out after being funnelled through a natural "panhandle" caused by *geological faults*. Half the delta is permanent swamp, the rest floods during the rainy season and is grassland at other times. The Okavango is a popular tourist destination because it is home to a rich variety of wildlife, including Africa's largest elephant population and more than 400 species of birds.

The Wadden Sea is Europe's largest tidal wetland. Protected from the North Sea by the Friesian Islands, the Wadden Sea stretches 310 miles (500 km) along the coasts of the Netherlands, Germany and Denmark. It is a combination of islands, sandbanks, salt marshes and tidal flats, covering a total area of 3,800 square miles (10,000 sq. km). The area is a vital stopover place for migrating birds and fish.

How Wetlands Change

A wetland is constantly undergoing change—growing, shrinking, or altering shape. These changes are affected by the amount of water entering or leaving the wetland and the amount of material carried by the water. Other changes are governed by plant growth and chemical reactions.

Rivers and streams are forever carving and shaping their own beds and edges, removing soil from their banks and carrying it downstream. In addition they also carry material washed down into them by rainfall. The bigger the river, the more sediment it carries. A flooding river can deposit millions of tons of soil over its floodplain. When it reaches the sea the river deposits all its remaining sediment. Deltas are built as these sediments are gradually spread along the coast to either side of the river's mouth.

In most wetlands, the amount of water changes with the seasons. In some places the river floodplains may show no sur-

Oxbow Lakes

In wide, shallow valleys rivers flow slowly, looping back and forth in a wandering, snake-like path. These snaking curves are called "meanders," after the River Menderes in Turkey. Meanders are formed as erosion wears away the outside of a bend, while eroded material from upstream is deposited on the inside of the bend, emphasizing the curve. Sometimes the neck of one of these loops is eroded away completely, creating a new, straighter course for the river. The old river loop becomes what is known as an oxbow lake. Cut off from the rest of the river, the oxbow lake may eventually dry up altogether.

This aerial photo shows several oxbow lakes that formed when the river changed its course due to the buildup of sediment.

With regular inflows of both fresh river water and seawater, the channels and mudflats of a river estuary are constantly changing. These areas are home to many small animals, such as crabs, as well as birds and other animals that feed on them.

face water for most of the year, but are temporarily covered with water when seasonal rains or melting snow cause the rivers to overflow. The permanent swamps of the Sudd region of Sudan cover up to 7,700 square miles (20,000 square kilometers), but during the rainy season the White Nile River overflows into the floodplain surrounding the swamps, and adds an additional 5,800 square miles (15,000 sq. km) to the wetland area.

In some floodplains the water largely disappears between rainy seasons. During the annual *monsoon* rains in Australia's

Northern territory and in Queensland, a number of large streams appear, and flood extensive areas. After the rains have departed, these floods evaporate and sink into the ground, leaving a few swamps and the waterholes known as billabongs.

Tidal Wetlands

Many rivers flood once or twice each year, but some types of wetland flood much more often. The rise and fall of the tides covers and uncovers many coastal wetlands twice a day, particularly in and around estuary mouths and deltas, where rivers meet the sea. Sandbanks, mudflats, islands, and salt marshes appear and disappear in coastal wetlands. They are continually changing shape and size as the tides rise and fall. These areas are subject to waves and storm surges as well as regular flooding.

The Mekong Delta of Southeast Asia, for example, consists of some 21,200 square miles (55,000 sq. km) of freshwater swamp forests, tidal mudflats, and mangroves. After the monsoon rains, floodwater rushing down the river meets with seawater surging upstream. The result is a temporary flood area of up to 131,000 square miles (340,000 sq. km).

Lakes and Bogs

While sediment deposits are constantly changing rivers and streams, deposits of a different sort can sometimes change lakes into marshes, or marshes into bogs. The process is known as succession. At first mud, gradually washed into a lake by streams, or eroded from the banks, settles on the lake bottom. Eventually the lake is shallow enough for plants that have

Bogs are often short of the nutrients needed by most plants. Certain plants, such as the sundew shown here, have evolved to survive bog conditions by trapping insects and digesting the nutrients contained in their bodies.

floating leaves and flowers to take root. More mud gathers around the roots of these plants, and the lake becomes even shallower. Other plants, known as emergents, take root around the margins. These have most of their stems above water, and are typical marsh plants.

Over the years silt, and increasing amounts of dead plant material, continue to build up. The new layers begin to solidify, becoming peat, which eventually takes over the whole lake area and turns it into a peat bog.

The decomposition of plant material in marshy areas is a major natural source of methane gas, which contributes towards global warming.

Waterlogging, high acidity, and low oxygen levels are all conditions favorable to peat formation. Such conditions hold back natural decomposition so that it cannot keep up with the amount of material accumulating.

In upland terrains many bogs are created not on overgrown lakes, but on wet, acidic soils. They are formed by remarkable plants called bog mosses, which can grow on waterlogged ground. These mosses hold on to large amounts of water. This water has absorbed acids from the underlying soil, and the mosses make it more acid by digesting the nutrients in it.

Text-Dependent Questions

1. What are some of the different types of wetlands?
2. How is an oxbow lake formed?
3. What is the world's largest inland delta?
4. How are peat bogs formed?

Research Project

Select one of the major types of wetlands. Using your school library or the internet, do some research. Where are these wetlands located, and what are some of the characteristics? Write a two-page report that details your findings and present it to your class.

 Words to Understand

amphibian—vertebrates (animals with backbones) that spend some time on land but need water in which to breed and grow to adulthood.

bacteria—microscopic single-celled living things. Some types are responsible for decay.

caiman—a South American reptile, similar to a crocodile or alligator.

gharial—a fish-eating Indian crocodile.

larva—the immature early stage of an insect, amphibian, or fish.

mollusc—an invertebrate (an animal without a backbone) with a soft body, usually having a shell.

navigable—a river or stretch of water along which large boats or ships can travel.

prey—an animal that is hunted for food by another animal.

rapids—fast, shallow river waters, usually running over rocks.

spawn—the egg mass of a fish or amphibian. The laying of these eggs is called spawning.

Every year many salmon leave the sea and move up rivers to spawn, swimming and leaping their way up torrents and rapids to reach the upper shallows.

Life in Wetlands

Wetlands are among the world's most vital habitats for plants and wildlife. From tiny insects and fish *larvae*, to birds and large mammals, many wild animal species are totally dependent on wetlands. Many plants, from microscopic floating species to forest trees, also need wetland conditions in order to survive.

Different plants grow in different parts of a wetland. Free-floating plants, such as duckweeds, colonize open areas of still water such as ponds and lakes, deriving all their nutrients from the water. Closer to the shore are plants such as waterweed, which root on the bottom but remain totally submerged. Closer again to the shore is a wide range of bottom-rooting plants with leaves and flowers which float on the surface of the water. These include water lilies and water hyacinths.

The plants of the water margins have their roots in the water or in waterlogged soil, and carry their flowers and seed-

Educational Video

Scan here for a video on the benefits of Florida's wetlands:

heads at the top of long stems. They include reeds, rushes, grasses and sedges.

Certain plants have adapted to life in wetlands that are low in nutrients by becoming meat-eaters. For example, sundews use sticky hairs to catch their insect *prey*, and the hairs move inwards to hold and digest the insect once it is stuck. Bladderworts are the largest and most widespread group of carnivorous plants. Scattered along the plant's stems and leaves are hundreds or thousands of tiny bladder-like traps, which catch insects and other small creatures.

Trees in Water

Some trees have developed special ways of surviving with their roots permanently in the water. The swamp cypress of North America often grows in permanently flooded areas, and has large, knee-like extensions to its underwater roots, which rise up out of the water around the trunk. The "knees" trap sediments, to create a solid supporting buttress that stops the tree from toppling over.

Mangrove trees also have arching prop roots to support them, but they have other problems to deal with. The mud that they grow in is usually very salty and contains very little oxygen. Some mangrove species get rid of extra salt through their leaves, while others have special cells in the roots that stop the salt being taken up with the water. Some mangrove species get extra oxygen through tiny pores (holes) in their prop roots. Others send up vertical root growths, which are breathing organs, into the air around the main trunk.

Underwater Creatures in Wetlands

Forty-one percent of all fish species are found in fresh water, even though fresh water covers only about 1 percent of the Earth's surface.

A great many fish take part in *spawning* migrations: they are born in one wetland area, they migrate to another area as

Mangroves grow in muddy tidal flats along many tropical coasts, and have developed unique ways of dealing with their marine environment The photo shows the wide spread of stilt-like roots that support the trees in the tidal mud, and the special breathing roots poking out of the mud into the air.

adults, but then return to their spawning grounds (the area where they were born) to breed. Many Mekong *species*, for instance, including the giant Mekong catfish, move from the main river into tributaries, swimming upstream to lay and fertilize their eggs in quiet shallows.

Some types of fish travel between fresh water wetlands and saltwater oceans. Salmon leave the sea to breed in the freshwater rivers where they were spawned. On the east coast of North America large shoals of alewives, a type of herring, enter estuaries and swim up rivers and streams to breed in ponds.

Freshwater eels spawn in the seaweed beds of the Sargasso Sea in the Atlantic Ocean. They make long journeys to leave the sea for rivers, where they live for 30 years or more. Eels can survive for long periods out of water, protected by a coat of slime. This enables them to wriggle between wetland sites overland. Eventually they return to the Sargasso Sea to breed.

Tidal wetlands such as estuaries and mangrove forests are important breeding sites and nurseries for some marine creatures.

Dragonflies are common wetland insects. Female dragonflies lay their eggs on or near the water surface. Adult dragonflies hunt above the water, but their larvae live beneath the surface, where they ambush tadpoles and small fish.

The vulnerable larvae and immature young of many species of fish and other marine creatures grow up in tidal wetlands. They provide many hiding places where these creatures can avoid predators until they grow large enough to enter deeper waters.

Mangroves thrive in a *bacteria*-rich mud. The bacteria help decompose fallen mangrove leaves to form a thick, nutritious layer that feeds fishes, prawns and other creatures. The wastes of these creatures in turn feed *molluscs* such as clams and water snails.

Freshwater Insects

Dragonflies and many other flying insects, including mosquitoes, lay their eggs in water or on the stems of water plants. The larvae that hatch from the eggs live underwater, sometimes for as long as two years, before emerging and changing into adults. Other insects, including several species of beetle, live permanently underwater. They breathe by capturing air from the surface and storing it under their wing-cases.

Water spiders need to breathe air, but they live and catch their prey underwater. They survive by making bell-shaped silk nets in which they capture air from the surface. They then anchor the nets to plant stems underwater. Water spiders also lay their eggs in these nets, and use them for storing prey. In Europe the spiders live in ponds and ditches containing plenty of weeds, often in peaty upland regions.

Amphibians

Wetlands are ideal habitats for *amphibians*. The word *amphibian* means "double life," because most species spend the first part of their life beneath the water surface, and much of their adult life on land (though they usually stay close to water). The most common amphibians are frogs and toads, but the group also includes newts, salamanders, and a group of legless amphibians called caecilians, which look like eels or large worms.

The tadpoles of wetland frogs and newts hatch from eggs laid in jelly-like envelopes in the water (frogspawn or newt spawn). The tadpoles have gills, which allow them to breathe underwater. The tadpoles gradually change (metamorphose) into adults, which have lungs for breathing air. A common frog tadpole starts to gulp air from the surface at 8 to 10 weeks old, and leaves the water at about 16 weeks.

Even as adults amphibians can survive for long periods underwater, as they can take in a certain amount of oxygen through their thin, moist skin. The need to keep this flexible skin moist is one of the things that makes wetlands perfect habitats for amphibians.

Reptiles

Reptiles such as crocodiles and turtles are among the planet's most successful species, and their success is due to their perfect adaptation to the wetlands they inhabit. Both turtles and crocodiles survived the global catastrophe that made the dinosaurs extinct millions of years ago, and both species have lived ever since in swamps, rivers, ponds, and lakes.

The crocodile family includes alligators, *caimans* (a group of south American species), and *gharials* (fish-eating crocodiles with long, thin snouts). All of them have nostrils and eyes

Crocodiles are efficient water-based predators. They hunt their prey, or lie in ambush for it, either underwater, or almost totally concealed just beneath the surface.

placed high on their skulls so that they can lay submerged but still watch for prey. Most live in warm climates, but some survive in cold waters in northern India and Nepal. These cold-water species sleep on river beds to avoid the coldest weather. They slow down their body processes, only surfacing now and then to breathe.

Some *aquatic* turtles swim, and some walk along the bottom. All breathe with lungs, but they are also able to some extent to take in oxygen through their skins while they are submerged. Some species spend the winter underwater, and may not surface to breathe for weeks at a time.

Most snakes are good swimmers, and many enter water in pursuit of frogs and other prey. Some are semi-aquatic. The American cottonmouth moccasin lives in lowland swamps and streams, and feeds mainly on fish and amphibians. Some snakes hunt larger prey in rivers and swamps. The South American anaconda preys on caimans and turtles as well as mammals and birds, and can reach over 10m in length.

Birds

Wetlands are essential to millions of water birds. Many species of geese, ducks and shorebirds breed on the lakes and wetlands of northern Europe and Asia. As winter approaches and insect

Migrating waterbirds such as these geese depend on extensive wetlands. They need them both as breeding areas, and as stopover sites where they can rest and feed during their migration flights.

food supplies dwindle, huge flocks of birds migrate along long-established flyways to warmer regions in southern Europe, southern Asia and Africa. Many stop over at wetland sites along the route, such as the French Camargue marshes, and the delta of the River Danube, to rest and feed before continuing their journey. Similar flocks migrate between the *tundra* areas of North America and warmer parts of South America.

Birds have adapted in a multitude of ways to wetland existence. Many, such as ducks, geese and swans, have webbed feet to aid swimming. The long necks of swans enable them to reach food on the bottom up to three feet (1 meter) below the surface. Birds such as oystercatchers and curlews probe mud and sand for worms and shellfish. Different species have beaks of different lengths, depending on how deep their prey lives.

Many birds of prey hunt in wetlands. Some hunt other wetland birds, but some, such as fishing eagles and ospreys, have developed techniques for snatching fish from near the surface.

Mammals in Wetlands

Few wetland mammals spend their entire lives in the water. Some that do include manatees and dugongs. Both species are distant relatives of elephants. These slow-moving plant-eaters have flippers and live in warm coastal shallows and rivers in the Americas and West Africa.

Freshwater dolphins are also completely aquatic. They are found in some Indian, Chinese, and South American rivers. River dolphins are smaller than their marine relatives, and they have longer snouts. The water in the rivers where these dolphins live is very cloudy, so the dolphins do not rely on eyesight to get around and find food. They get around using echolocation ("seeing" using sound), and find fishes and crabs by probing the mud with their snouts.

Some mammals are considered to be semi-aquatic, meaning they need to live near water. Hippos, the largest of the semi-aquatic mammals, spend their days in water, where they also mate and give birth. But at night they leave their rivers to feed on vegetation. Capybaras are the South American equivalents of hippos.

Otters and beavers spend most of their lives in the water. Both species have webbed feet and are excellent swimmers. The beaver actually alters the nature of wetlands, by damming streams to create large ponds or lakes.

Several mammals hunt fish in the shallows of rivers, including jaguars and bears. The flat-headed cat of Southeast Asia is particularly adapted to the fish-eating life. It has a flat skull, very small ears, long, sharp upper teeth, and webbed toes. It is found in swamps, marshes, lakes, and forests flanking rivers. It feeds on fish, frogs, and shrimps, and puts its head completely underwater to snatch prey.

Humans Living in Wetlands

Very few people in today's world live in close harmony with wetland environments. This is because the wetlands themselves have been reduced or changed by modern technology. However, some communities still survive and live much as they have done for centuries, though most are under threat.

Lake Titicaca is in the Andes mountains on the border between Bolivia and Peru. At over 12,500 feet (3800 m) above

A village built on an island made from matted reeds floats on Lake Titicaca, on the border between Peru and Bolivia. Communities such as this depend on wetland resources.

sea level, it is the highest *navigable* lake on Earth. The lake is the home and the means of living for communities of native fishermen, hunters and herders, some of whom live on floating islands of matted vegetation in the lake. They keep cattle, vicuñas (a type of llama), and sheep on the shore.

They catch fish to eat and to sell, using boats made from bundles of the reeds that grow in large beds around the lake. Their houses are also made from reeds, and they use reeds to make handicrafts, which they sell. The way of life of these lake dwellers is beginning to change, and many now make most of their money by renting out rooms to tourists.

On the other side of the world, the Marsh Arabs of Iraq also build boats and houses from reeds, and live on artificial floating islands. For 5,000 years they have lived among the marshes and lakes of southern Iraq, fishing for food. In recent years the fishermen have begun to switch from spears to nets, in order to catch more fish. They then sell the surplus fish in nearby towns.

The Marsh Arabs also now prefer wooden or metal boats to reed boats. In recent decades their way of life has been greatly threatened. After the 1991 Gulf War in Iraq, the government of Saddam Hussein diverted river water from the marshes for irrigation projects. Subsequently, the wetlands where the Marsh Arabs lived shrank by approximately 90 percent. Saddam's government also attacked Marsh Arab villages, because they sometimes protected those who dissented from his regime. But after the US-led invasion of Iraq that overthrew Saddam's government in the spring of 2003, the Marsh Arabs destroyed through some of the dams and dykes that were diverting the water. Since then the wetlands have begun to recover, although they are still only about half the size that they were in the mid-1970s.

Thai River Villages

Another community of wetland dwellers whose way of life is threatened live in Thailand along the Mekong River and its tributaries. The lives of local villagers are closely bound up with the seasonal cycles of the river and the hundreds of species of fish in it. Before each fishing season the villagers perform religious ceremonies at favorite fishing spots. In April and May, until recently the prize catch was always the giant catfish, caught as it swam upstream to spawn. These fish could weigh up to 660 pounds (300 kg). However dams, and the dynamiting of rocky *rapids*, mean that these catfish are threatened with extinction.

The villagers are also greatly dependant on wild plants and on vegetables cultivated in river-bank gardens and on mounds and small islands in the water. Over 100 local plants are used as herbs and for food. Some people make their living by gathering these plants and selling them.

Dams have already seriously affected water levels and movements of fish up the river. New plans to blast channels through rapids, to make it possible for boats to navigate the river, could disrupt traditional village life forever.

Text-Dependent Questions

1. What are some plants that grow at the margins of the water?
2. How do tidal wetlands provide important breeding sites for some marine creatures?
3. What are some reptile species that live in wetlands?

Research Project

Do some research on wetland plants, using your school library or the internet. What are some ways that these plants have adapted to survive? How do they spread their seeds, or protect themselves from being eaten? Write a two-page report and share your findings with the class.

 Words to Understand

basin—a bowl-shaped dip or depression in the ground.

pollution—the process of harming a natural area of soil, air or water with chemicals or waste products.

toxic—poisonous.

transpiration—the process by which plants lose water from their leaves.

The Benefits of Wetlands

Wetlands do not exist in isolation from the rest of the environment. They protect the land from the destructive force of seasonal floods and chemical build-ups, delivering nutrients to benefit plants and animals downstream, and producing crops of foods and materials.

Wetlands take the pressure off rivers, especially during times of seasonal rains and thaws, which can overload river channels. Marshes, swamps, and lakes within the natural drainage *basin* of a river are filled up in wet seasons. They hold a great deal of water that would otherwise drain into the main river channel and cause flooding.

Eventually the wetlands release the extra water. Some may sink into the ground and becomes groundwater, held by underground rocks. Some may flow through the rock layers to enter other wetlands downstream. Some evaporates from wetland surfaces and becomes water vapor. Water also evaporates from the leaves of wetland plants—a process known as *transpiration*.

A river's floodwaters may eventually reach regions of natural floodplain where they overflow the river's banks, but the "sponge" effect of upstream wetlands help to keep these floods to manageable levels.

How Wetlands Trap Pollution

Wetlands can be effective traps for sediments. The sediments may be soil and rock particles eroded from hillsides and stream banks by heavy rain, or they may be the broken topsoils of agricultural land. River basin marshes and bogs are like shallow bowls with built-in filters and sponges. They trap sediments as they are carried towards the river in streams and flowing surface water. This helps prevent the river having to carry too great a sediment load of its own, which could raise its bed and contribute to flooding.

The sediments that build up on the wetland floor can trap *pollutants* from factories and from farming. The pollutants become attached to particles of sediment, where they may gradually lose their harmful qualities.

Some poisonous heavy metals, such as copper, lead, and cadmium, may be absorbed and trapped by sedges (coarse grasses), bulrushes, cattails and

Educational Video

For a video on how wetlands can fight pollution, scan here:

Deforestation can expose land to severe erosion. Seasonal rains wash huge quantities of earth down hillsides, producing deep rain channels. Wetlands can help to absorb some of the sediments resulting from erosion, which would otherwise clog up the river channel.

other wetland plants. The bacteria in wetland soils are also able to make some heavy metals non-*toxic*.

How Wetlands Help Farmers

As plants die off, they release many of the nutrients that have been feeding them back into the soil. Seasonal rains carry soil and nutrients into streams and rivers, which ferry them downstream. Many rivers have natural floodplains, where regular floodwaters spread across flat riverside land. Each time the land floods, soil particles mixed with plant nutrients are

Rice needs a wet environment to thrive, and is planted throughout Asia in artificially flooded rice fields, or paddies. These rice paddies are in Japan.

deposited as a layer of silt. The silt remains on the land as the floods recede, and enriches the soil. Rice is a major floodplain crop, and the main food of more than three billion people worldwide. Other food-producing wetland plants include coconut and oil palms, and the sago palm, which provides the basic food of many Southeast Asian communities.

Apart from food, wetland plants can provide local people with a renewable supply of wood for building and fuel, as well as bark for leather tanning.

Wetland animals that serve as protein foods include fish—both wild-caught and farmed—waterbirds, mammals like the South American capybara, and reptiles such as alligators, which are hunted or bred for meat.

The Benefit to Grazing Animals

Floodplain grasslands provide vital grazing for both wild and domestic animals. On the floodplains of the Okavango Delta in Botswana, dry winter grasses grow on land that is flooded in the rainy season. These grasses are nourished by silt left behind from the floods. The grasses attract massive herds of large grazing mammals such as buffaloes, zebras, wildebeest, and impalas.

The giant Amazon water lily has leaves that can reach nearly seven feet (2 meters) across, and can support a weight of over 100 pounds (45 kg) without sinking.

Tribesmen herd cattle in South Sudan, near the vast swamp known as the Sudd.

In the Sudd Marshes, which are within the floodplain of the White Nile, rich wetland grasses grow on the floodplain each year once the floods have receded. For many generations, herdspeople of the Dinka tribe have grazed their cattle on these grasses.

How Wetlands Protect Coasts

Flood sediments carried down to estuaries and tidal flats provide essential nutrients for the many marine species that use them as nurseries. These wetlands provide relatively well protected shallow waters where the young of marine species can develop, with less danger of being eaten by predators than in the open sea.

Molluscs such as oysters, clams and mussels, and crustaceans such as crabs and shrimp, depend on tidal wetlands as breeding and feeding habitats.

There are almost 80 species of plants known as mangroves, and mangrove forests cover an area of some 70,000 square miles (180,000 sq. km) worldwide.

Wetland plants stabilize banks and shorelines, and bear the brunt of storms from the sea, reducing their power as they travel inland. The mangrove forests that occur along many tropical coasts provide important sea defenses in regions where powerful storm surges are a real danger to low-lying coastal communities.

Text-Dependent Questions

1. How do wetlands take pressure off of rivers?
2. How do wetlands trap toxic metals and other pollution?
3. What are some ways that wetlands help farmers?
4. What are the benefits of wetlands to grazing animals?

Research Project

Mangrove trees play an important role in protecting the coastal wetlands of Florida and Louisiana. Using the internet or your school library, find out more about recent efforts to protect mangroves. Write a two-page report on your findings, and share it with your class.

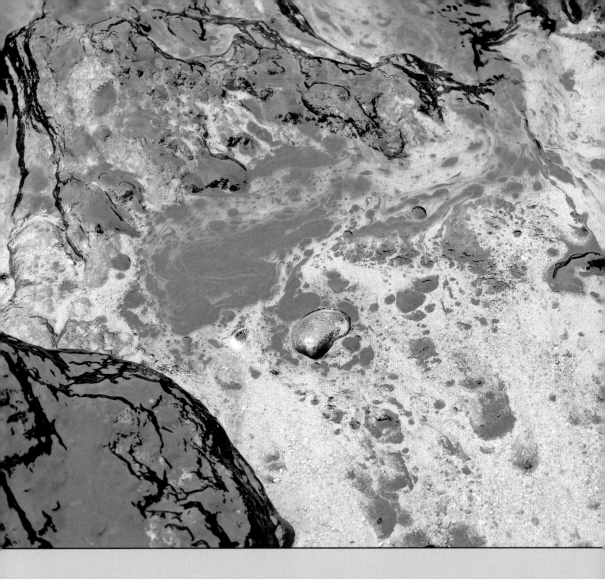

 Words to Understand

algae—tiny, aquatic, plant-like organisms that sometimes blanket the surface of stagnant (still) or slow-flowing water.

fertilizer—a substance added to soil to help plants to grow.

pesticide—a poison used to kill weeds, or insects and other crop pests.

sluice-gate—a gate that controls water flow through an opening in a dam.

4

The Threat to Wetlands

In the past, wetlands have had a bad public image. They were seen as wastelands, full of disease and danger. For centuries governments have drained, levelled, and developed wetland areas for non-wetland uses such as intensive agriculture or the expansion of towns and industries. This "land reclamation" is still the biggest threat to wetlands.

Today, wetlands cover roughly 6 percent of the Earth's land area. This is about half the area that they originally covered. Most wetland loss has occurred since 1900. The worst losses occurred in northern countries during the first half of the 20th century but since 1950 tropical and subtropical wetlands have been lost at an increasing rate.

Drainage and clearance to make room for agriculture has been the main cause of wetland destruction. Some scientists estimate that by 1985 up to 65 percent of available wetlands in Europe and North America had been drained to make way for intensive agriculture. In Asia, the figure was 27 percent; in South America 6 percent, and in Africa 2 percent.

In the United States, according to the US National Oceanic and Atmospheric Administration (NOAA), more than half of all the wetlands in the lower 48 states have been destroyed since the 1700s. Wetland destruction has been almost total in some states. California, Ohio, Indiana, Illinois, Missouri, and Iowa have lost over 85 percent of their original wetlands. Seventeen other states, including Florida and Louisiana, have lost approximately half of their original wetland areas. States that border the Gulf of Mexico have the highest sustained wetland loss rate in the country. At the same time, many of the willow wetlands of the Rocky Mountains have given way to cattle grazing, housing developments, ski resorts, and agriculture. According to a recent study by the US Fish and Wildlife Service, America's wetlands are disappearing at a rate of about 80,000 acres (32,400 hectares) every year.

Poisoning Wetlands

Wetlands can filter out or nullify many chemicals that drain into them. However, massive pollution from farms can kill wetlands. A large proportion of the *fertilizers* used by farmers to increase their crop yields eventually drain off their fields and are washed downstream to enter bogs, marshes, and lakes.

The nitrogen and phosphorus in this agricultural runoff stimulate the growth of plant-like organisms called *algae*—a process called eutrophication. The masses of algae cover the surface of standing or slow-moving water with a dense green blanket. This blocks off the light needed by more useful water

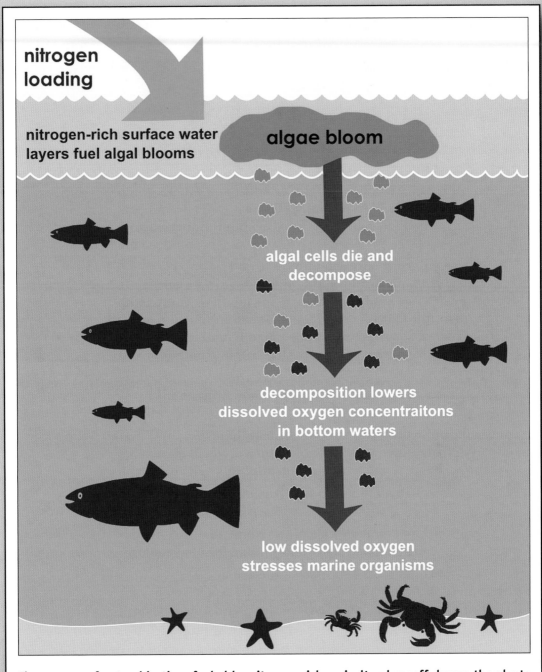

nitrogen loading

nitrogen-rich surface water layers fuel algal blooms

algae bloom

algal cells die and decompose

decomposition lowers dissolved oxygen concentraitons in bottom waters

low dissolved oxygen stresses marine organisms

The process of eutrophication, fueled by nitrogen-rich agricultural runoff, harms the plants and wildlife of wetlands.

Cranberries are a natural wetland plant, but commercial cranberry farms use large amounts of chemicals and heavy harvesting machinery, which exclude natural wildlife from the cranberry bogs.

plants. When the algae die and decompose, they remove the water's oxygen, so that it can support little plant or animal life.

Pesticides, and many household and industrial cleaners, contain chemicals that enter sewage and drainage systems, and find their way into wetlands, rivers, and finally the sea. Many of these chemicals were designed to kill pests or bacteria, and can be very harmful to aquatic animals.

Massive quantities of human sewage wastes can also overcome a wetland's natural cleaning capacities. The Lac de Tunis, outside the Tunisian capital, and the Manzalah lagoon outside Cairo have become cesspits for these major cities. Both are filled with stagnant water clogged with algae and able to support hardly any other life forms.

Hydroelectric Dams and Wetlands

Modern cities and industries need huge supplies of electricity to keep them going. They also use huge supplies of water, as do the farms that grow food to feed the urban populations. Large dams and hydroelectric generation are an obvious way of meeting these demands. Hydroelectricity provides about 16 percent of the world's electricity, according to the International Energy Agency.

Today, more than 50,000 large dams have been built on rivers throughout the world. (A large dam is defined as being higher than 50 feet/15 meters.) These dams are constructed for many reasons, such as producing hydroelectric power, creating reservoirs of drinking water, irrigation for farm fields, or flood prevention. A 2016 report by the World Wildlife Fund (WWF) found that more than 60 percent of the world's 227 largest rivers have been impacted by dams. The WWF report found that damming of rivers has led to a decline in freshwater animal species, displacement of human populations, and the destruction of wetlands.

In a large river system such as the Mekong River, the effects

Educational Video

To learn how hydroelectric power is generated, scan here:

of dams are felt far upstream and downstream. Upstream, water levels rise to cover wetlands such as swamps, marshes and river islands. Fish migrations are blocked, and damage is done to wildlife. Downstream, flooding depends on the opening or closing of the dam's *sluices*.

While dams do provide human communities with protection from unpredictable river flooding, they also eliminate the restoration of nutrients to farmlands. This means that farmers must use more chemical fertilizers to grow their crops. This increases the chemical runoff that enters wetlands, leading to algae growth and eutrophication.

For example, Egypt's High Aswan Dam holds back the Nile waters. The nutritious silts once deposited annually by the river across its floodplain are now trapped in the artificial lake

The Loss of Mangrove Forests

Mangrove forests are one of the world's most threatened tropical ecosystems. Over 35 percent of the world's mangroves have disappeared over the past three decades. The figure is as high as 50 percent in countries such as India, the Philippines, Indonesia, Thailand, and Vietnam, while in the Americas they are being cleared at a rate faster than tropical rainforests.

Mangrove forests have been bulldozed to make room for marinas, hotels, airports, rice paddies, and shrimp ponds. Shrimp farming has become a major industry in Asia, providing food for millions of people. In countries like the Philippines, Bangladesh, Guatemala, Honduras, and Ecuador, mangrove forests were replaced them with shrimp ponds. In the process, however, the people destroyed their coastal storm defenses, removed the rich mud that nurtured many marine creatures, and lost trees that delivered regular annual supplies of useful products.

The artificial lakes which form behind large dams, such as this one in Portugal, permanently flood wetland systems upstream.

behind the dam. Also, the reduced flow of the river below the dam allows seawater to get into groundwater in the Nile Delta, which further damages the natural wetlands. The loss of silt has also affected Egypt's major sardine fisheries beyond the Nile Delta, and the delta itself is rapidly shrinking. Traditional brick manufacturers, who used to use flood silt to make bricks, have had to move onto agricultural lands to excavate silts now that the floods have ceased.

Dams also tend to displace human communities in what were formerly wetland areas, as water backs up behind the dam to create large reservoirs. According to the Global Freshwater Program in the United States, up to 80 million people worldwide have been displaced by the construction of large

The generating room of a hydroelectric power station. Hydroelectric power is a clean way of generating electricity. It has benefited many countries by producing power for homes and industries.

dams, while an estimated 470 million people living down-stream have had their lives affected in a negative way by the dam's construction. These people are uprooted, and often have to move to other areas to find work. They rarely benefit from the electricity generated by the dams, most of which is sold to industry or goes to major towns.

The Effect on Wetland Wildlife

Animals that have adapted to wetland lifestyles are especially at risk from wetland degradation because of their adaptations.

Without suitable wet conditions in which to breed, amphibians and wetland reptiles cannot survive. Also, migrating water-birds need wetlands as stopover points on their long flights for rest and food.

The effect of pollution on wetland wildlife is not always direct. Pesticides that are washed into wetlands strike first at the bottom of food chains, entering microscopic plant and animal organisms. Filter-feeding creatures such as worms and shellfish are the next in line, absorbing the long-lasting chemicals from the plankton on which they feed. Fish and birds feed on the worms and shellfish. At the top end of wetland food chains, birds of prey, dolphins, and seals feed on waterbirds and fish, and the entire accumulated load of poisons becomes lodged in their body fats and organs. The results can seriously affect their ability to breed, with birds of prey laying sterile eggs, and mammals dying from diseases because the chemicals damage their immune systems.

Oil spills and illegal oil discharges are another threat to mangroves and the wildlife that is depend on them. Oil clogs the trees' breathing pores, and the roots become starved of oxygen. As the trees die off, they cease to provide the leaf-litter that mud bacteria need to make nutrients. Without the nutrients, fish and other marine creatures and their larvae cannot survive.

Oil spills have occurred in the Gulf of Mexico, most notably the Deepwater Horizon offshore drilling rig disaster in April 2010 which spilled more than 210 million gallons of oil into the Gulf. Cleanup of the oil, which washed onto about 1,100 miles (1,700 km) of coastline in Louisiana, Mississippi, Alabama, and Florida, took years and cost billions of dollars; the long-term effect on fish, wildlife, and plants of the coastal wetlands is still being studied.

There have also been oil pipeline failures far from the coasts that have damaged wetlands. In 2010, a ruptured oil pipeline contaminated 40 miles (64 km) of Michigan's Kalamazoo River and surrounding wetlands. In 2013, another pipeline broke in a small Arkansas town called Mayflower, causing a major spill that affected nearby wetlands. And in 2017, the state of North Dakota reported that there had been 745 oil spills from pipelines within the previous year—an average of one oil spill every 11 hours and 45 minutes.

Industrial pollution sometimes leads to a total breakdown of wetland life systems. Smoke from industrial chimneys in parts of northern Europe mixes with rain clouds to fall as acid rain elsewhere on the continent. Over a fifth of Sweden's larger lakes now have a high acid content, and many Scandinavian lakes are crystal clear, because they are totally without plant or animal life. Living things cannot survive in the acid water.

Threatened Wetland Animals

According to the World Conservation Union (IUCN), over 800 animal species with close ties to wetlands are currently threatened with extinction. Wetland species cannot easily adapt to new environments.

In 1979 a large sea fish called the totoaba, native to the Gulf of California on the Pacific coast of North America, was declared endangered. The totoaba depended on the delta of the Colorado River, breeding in the mouth of the river. Tides carried the eggs up into the delta where they hatched. Unfortunately, almost all the waters of the river are now diverted for irrigation, leaving only a trickle at the river mouth. Another species that is dependant on the delta, and becoming rarer, is vaquita porpoise, the world's most endangered marine mammal. The population of these animals has fallen from an estimated 600 in 1997 to about 30 porpoises by 2017. Other endangered wildlife in this region includes the brown pelican and the delta clam.

The Florida panther, a subspecies of the cougar lives in the swamp forests of the Florida Everglades. It suffers from a shrinking habitat as humans take more and more of the land. Loss of habitat also reduces prey numbers, and panthers are killed in road accidents. Although conservation efforts have helped the Florida panther population rebound—there are about 230 panthers in 2017, up from an estimated 30 panthers in the early 1980s. However, the species is still endangered, as are other birds and animals native to the Everglades, such as the Everglades snail kite, American alligator, eastern indigo snake, and wood stork.

Depletion of Freshwater Fish

Humans annually consume 30 million tons of freshwater fish. Despite this dependence, many freshwater fish-stocks have been depleted through human activity, depriving fishing communities of both food and work. Pollution of wetlands as well as water diversion both contribute to the decline in numbers of freshwater fish.

A Florida panther in the Everglades. The panther is now close to extinction due to habitat loss and inbreeding. Panther support groups have had some success introducing panthers from outside the area to overcome the problems of inbreeding.

In the Everglades and elsewhere, the introduction of fish, animals, or plants that are not native to the wetlands have been catastrophic to native species. Trees like Melaleuca or Australian pines, which were planted in some areas as decorative windbreaks, have displaced many native trees and plants, and affected the habitats for birds. Exotic animals like the Burmese python prey on 39 endangered species and 41 additional rare species. Most were unwanted pets that were abandoned in the Everglades; the population has increased greatly to an estimated 5,000 or more. The Burmese python does not have natural predators in the Everglades, and they have been known to kill and eat alligators, the other top predator in the region.

Another example of an invasive species' effect on wetlands is that of the Nile perch, a large fish that can weigh up to 440 pounds (200 kg). In the 1950s large numbers of Nile perch were introduced into Africa's Lake Victoria, with the expectation that they would provide food for fishermen. However, the invasive Nile perch soon started eating the small fish that naturally lived in the lake. These fish were the basis of the fishing industry in the area. By the 1980s up to 200 species of native fish were extinct. The locals used to wind-dry the small fish, but this is impossible with the large perch. It has to be cooked in its own oil, using large amounts of firewood. Deforestation of islands and lake shores is occurring as a result. As the trees are cut down, larger quantities of topsoil, often laced with agricultural chemicals, erode into the waterways. This has a negative effect on animal and plant life, and as a result the Lake Victoria fisheries may collapse due to overfishing.

The Effect on Migratory Animals

Unexpected changes in wetland terrains can be both confusing and deadly for migrating animals. Dams block the breeding and feeding movements of both fish and river dolphins in the Irrawaddy and Yangtze rivers. Filled ponds and ditches can remove the spawning grounds of amphibians such as toads and frogs. Migrating waterbirds can fail to reach their breeding and feeding grounds if the wetlands they use as stopovers have disappeared.

Artificial obstacles such as this oil pipeline in the Alaskan Arctic may cut across the traditional migration routes of caribou herds, which travel thousands of miles north and south each year.

Man-made barriers can cause problems for wildlife. An incomplete canal bed across the Sudd Marshes produced a barrier that migrating grazers cannot cross. In the James Bay region of Quebec, Canada, 10,000 migrating caribou were drowned in 1984 when sluice gates were opened on a hydro-electric dam upstream of their migratory route.

The Effect on Humans

Housing, airports, electrical power, or farm fields seem far more important to growing human populations, desperate for space, than marshes or swamps. Unfortunately, changing a wetland into a human facility often solves one problem in the short term but creates a host of others in the long term.

The destruction or degradation of a wetland can totally disrupt the lives of those depending on it. The reservoirs of dams drown villages, and pollution can make wetlands uninhabitable, forcing wetland communities to move out.

Text-Dependent Questions

1. What is the biggest threat to wetlands?
2. What is eutrophication? How does it harm wetlands?
3. What are some reasons that dams are built on large rivers? How do dams affect wetland areas?

Research Project

There are dozens of invasive plant and animal species that are affecting the Florida Everglades. Choose one of these invasive species and find out more about it, using your school library or the internet. How and why was it introduced to the Everglades? What native species does it affect, and how does it affect them? Write a two-page report with your findings, and share it with your class.

Words to Understand

tributary—a stream or river which runs into a larger flow of water.

lobby—to express your point of view to the government or to other officials, and to encourage them to undertake actions that will support this view.

Protesters will go to great lengths to demonstrate their opposition to pipelines and dams when they realize that their entire way of life is under threat. These protesters in Portland, Oregon, are opposed to the Dakota Access Pipeline, which would threaten clean water used by Sioux living on the Standing Rock Indian Reservation.

Protecting Wetlands

Many people have been aware of the dangers facing wetlands for a long time, but there now seems to be a growing sense of urgency. An increasing number of organizations, many of them independent of governments, are doing research and giving publicity to the problems. In some countries local people have started to organize protests against projects such as dams.

The Ramsar Convention on Wetlands, set up in 1971, is an international conservation agreement. It brings governments and independent organizations together to consider wetland problems. One of its best-known activities is the establishing of particular Ramsar sites for governments to maintain and protect. All its recommendations are voluntary, and although there are 2,266 Ramsar sites worldwide, many remain at risk, with governments taking little or no protective action.

Independent organizations concerned with general wildlife

welfare, or with general environmental protection, often campaign on wetland issues. Probably the best known is the World Wildlife Fund (WWF), which was set up as a charity in 1961. WWF is one of the largest independent conservation organizations, operating in a hundred countries with over 5 million supporters.

Other independent organizations whose work covers wetland issues include the International Conservation Union (IUCN), Friends of the Earth, Greenpeace, the Royal Society for the Protection of Birds, and the Whale and Dolphin Conservation Society. All of these organizations issue large amounts of information and publicity through leaflets, magazine articles, and websites, as well as carrying out education programs and conservation activities in the field. On the whole, they remain free of the influence of governments and large corporations.

The United Nations has also worked to conserve wetlands worldwide, through its UN Environment Programme (UNEP). This agency helps developing countries to implement environ-

An Early Success

One of WWF's early campaigns was to raise money to buy a section of the Guadalquivir Marshes in Spain. This area was an important wetland habitat, and a stopover point for millions of migrating birds. In 1969, with the help of the Spanish Government, WWF bought the land and set up the Coto Doñana National Park, an important European wetland site. WWF is currently campaigning against the drainage of water from the marshes for irrigation and to service tourist facilities.

Dried freshwater fish being sold in a Thai market. Village life, based on small-scale production of food which is then sold locally, can enable villagers to live a productive and secure life. It also encourages a healthy environment.

mentally sound policies and practices. The United Nations Educational, Scientific and Cultural Organization (UNESCO) has designated some of the major wetlands areas as World Heritage Sites that deserve special protection. These include the Everglades, the Okavango Delta, and the Pantanal in South America.

Fighting the Governments

In many countries taking direct action against official policies is risky, but it sometimes works. For many years fishing communities in the Mekong Delta demonstrated, marched, and even occupied public buildings in their fight against the damming of the Mun *tributary*. The protesters were beaten, abused, and sometimes imprisoned. But ultimately, the authorities agreed to open the sluice gates of the dam during the fishes' breeding season. This allowed the migratory fish to pass through the dam to breed upstream. Soon, the villagers were able to catch fish again as they had for centuries.

 Educational Video

Scan here for a short video on the U.S. government's assessment of wetlands:

In the end, governments make the decisions, and some of their decisions have helped wetlands. Many countries banned the use of certain chemical pesticides, such as DDT, when it was discovered that their use was toxic to animals and posed a potential danger to humans as well. Governments have imposed stiff fines on oil companies that release oil into the sea or break safety regulations when it comes to pipelines. Unfortunately,

One area in which progress has been made in the fight to persuade governments to care for wetlands is the replanting of mangrove forests. Scientists and ecologists have come to understand that up to 90 percent of commercial fish stocks may

One of the best ways to ensure the survival of wetlands and other natural environments is to teach young people their importance by giving them first hand, on-site experience.

depend on healthy mangroves. In places like Pakistan, Bangladesh, Australia, Papua New Guinea, China, and the United States, conservation and replanting work has begun.

What the Future Holds

Where wetlands are concerned, all problems are urgent. Wildlife habitats are under threat and species are in danger of extinction. Human wetland communities are being displaced permanently, and their cultures disrupted. Freshwater supplies are dwindling while water demand is increasing.

Wetland campaigners continue to *lobby* governments and industry with scientific arguments showing why wetlands should be conserved or repaired. They also continue educating the public about wetland degradation. Meanwhile it is possible that a further argument, closer to politicians' hearts, will make an impact. Wetland destruction costs governments money. Some of these costs are obvious. Cleaning up a major oil spill is expensive, but has to be done because of the tourist industry as well as the wildlife. Dams cost a fortune to build, and sometimes do not produce enough electricity to cover their costs.

Environmental refugees present another sort of financial burden. People who are moved to make way for a reservoir, or whose livelihood is destroyed by the draining of wetlands, flock to towns seeking jobs. The ever-increasing numbers of such refugees mean that cities need extra food, water, housing, jobs, transport and medical care. Faced with ever larger bills for keeping their cities running, governments may begin to think that it was better when villagers lived in self-supporting communities, growing their own vegetables, tending their own animals and catching their own fish. As villagers they created money, selling produce, fish and wild herbs. As environmental refugees they cost money.

The future for many wetlands is perilous. Politicians often do not have the time or the energy to think about rare deer or endangered trees. By themselves the rarities and the fragile habitats earn neither money nor votes.

But wetlands fit into a larger picture, and much of the information coming from scientists and teachers stresses that species and environments should be seen as parts of this larger whole. Everything has its role to play, and the health of the whole depends on the health of the parts.

 Text-Dependent Questions

1. What is the Ramsar Convention on Wetlands?
2. How does the United Nations help to protect wetlands?

 Research Project

The list of UNESCO World Heritage Sites can be found online at http://whc.unesco.org/en/list. It includes more than 200 natural sites, such as the Everglades or the Sundarbans wetlands. Choose one of these sites and do some research on it, using the internet or your school library. Why was the site chosen by UNESCO? How does preserving this natural area help humanity? What steps have been taken to protect the area. Write a two-page paper and present it to your class.

Quick Reference

Wetlands

A wetland is an area of land that is either covered with water or saturated with water for at least part of the year. Wetlands exist in many kinds of climates, on every continent except Antarctica. They vary in size from isolated prairie water holes to huge salt marshes. They are found along coasts and inland. Some wetlands are flooded woodlands, full of trees like mangroves. Others are more like flat, watery grasslands. Still others are choked by thick, spongy mosses.

Area of Freshwater Wetlands

1. **Central and South America**, 414,917,000 hectares (1,025,282,233 acres)
2. **North America**, 241,574,000 hectares (596,942,353 acres)
3. **Eastern Europe**, 229,217,000 hectares (556,407,541 acres)
4. **Asia**, 204,245,000 hectares (504,700,385 acres)
5. **Africa**, 121,322,000 hectares (299,793,190 acres)
6. **Oceania,** 35,750,000 hectares (88,340,173 acres)
7. **Western Europe,** 28,822,000 hectares (71,220,713 acres)
Total: 1,275,847,000 hectares (3,152,686,590 acres)

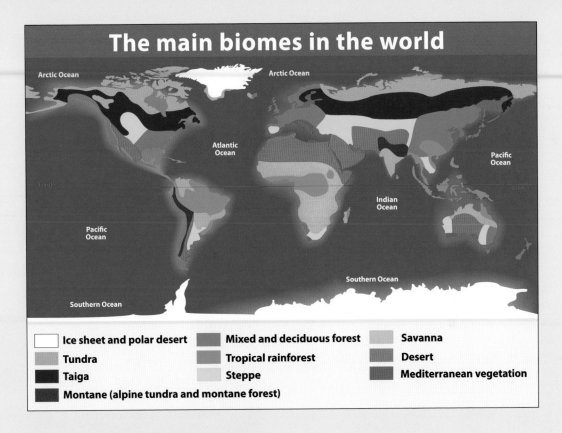

The main biomes in the world

Arctic Ocean

Arctic Ocean

Atlantic Ocean

Pacific Ocean

Equator

Indian Ocean

Pacific Ocean

Southern Ocean

Southern Ocean

- Ice sheet and polar desert
- Tundra
- Taiga
- Montane (alpine tundra and montane forest)
- Mixed and deciduous forest
- Tropical rainforest
- Steppe
- Savanna
- Desert
- Mediterranean vegetation

Facts about Wetlands

- Wetlands provide a valuable habitat for birds. About half of all North American bird species nest or feed in wetlands.
- Wetlands also are home to many endangered species. More than one-third of American endangered species rely directly or indirectly on wetlands for their survival.
- Wetlands are the first line of defense for flood control. An acre of wetland can store 1 million gallons of floodwater.
- Global consumption of fresh water is doubling every 20 years. Wetlands clean and purify groundwater, making it drinkable.
- About 95 percent of commercially harvested fish and shellfish depend on wetlands for food or as a safe place to hatch their young.

Appendix

Climate Change

The Earth's climate has changed throughout history. During the last 650,000 years there have been seven cycles of glacial advance and retreat. The end of the last ice age, about 11,700 years ago, marks the beginning of the modern climate era—and of human civilization.

Today, the Earth is experiencing another warming period. Since the 1950s scientists have found that average global temperatures have gradually risen by more than 1° Fahrenheit (0.6° Celsius). In the past, periods of warming and cooling have been attributed to very small variations in Earth's orbit that change the amount of solar energy our planet receives. Two things make the current warming trend unusual. First, most scientists agree that the warming is probably caused by human activities that release carbon dioxide into the atmosphere. Second, the speed at which the Earth's temperature is rising is much faster than this phenomenon has ever occurred in the past, according to climate records.

The heat-trapping nature of carbon dioxide and other "greenhouse gases" was demonstrated in the mid-19th century. Without the Earth's atmosphere, the sun's energy would be reflected back into space. Greenhouse gases in the atmosphere trap some of the sun's heat, reflecting it back to keep the earth's

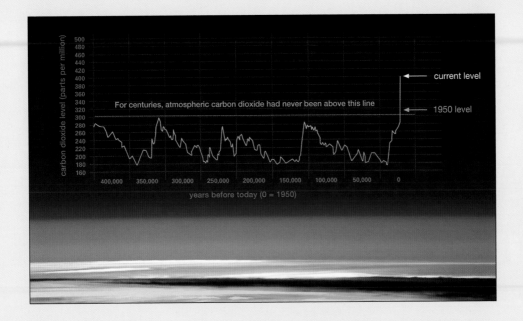

carbon dioxide level (parts per million)

For centuries, atmospheric carbon dioxide had never been above this line

current level

1950 level

years before today (0 = 1950)

surface warmer than it would otherwise be. Without the atmosphere, the Earth's average temperature would be 0°F (–18°C). Thanks to the greenhouse effect, Earth's average temperature is currently about 59°F (15°C).

Increased levels of greenhouse gases in the atmosphere must cause the Earth to warm in response. Since the start of the Industrial Revolution in the mid-eighteenth century, human activities—including the burning of "fossil fuels" like oil, coal, and natural gas, as well as farming and the clearing of large forested areas—have produced a 40 percent increase in the atmospheric concentration of carbon dioxide, from 280 parts per million (ppm) in 1750 to over 400 ppm today.

Scientists understand how the Earth's climate has changed over the past 650,000 years by studying ice cores drawn from Greenland, Antarctica, and tropical mountain glaciers. Varying

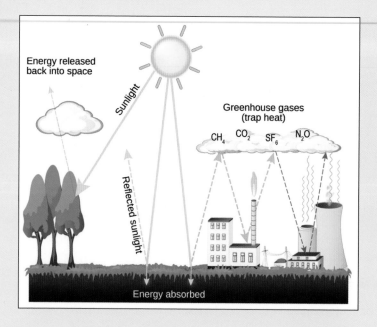

Energy released back into space

Sunlight

Greenhouse gases
(trap heat)

CH₄ CO₂ SF₆ N₂O

Reflected sunlight

Energy absorbed

carbon dioxide levels found in the ancient ice show how the Earth's climate responds to changes in greenhouse gas levels. Ancient evidence can also be found in tree rings, ocean sediments, coral reefs, and layers of sedimentary rocks. This ancient, or paleoclimate, evidence reveals that current warming is occurring roughly ten times faster than the average rate of ice-age-recovery warming.

Most scientists believe that if greenhouse gas emissions continue at the present rate, Earth's surface temperature could grow much warmer than it has been in more than 650,000 years. Recent studies indicate that, if emissions are not reduced, the Earth could warm by another 3.6°F (2°C) over the next twenty years. This would have an extremely harmful effect on ecosystems, biodiversity, and the livelihoods of people worldwide.

Evidence of Climate Change

Earth's average surface temperature has risen about 2°F (1.1°C) since the late nineteenth century. Most of this warming has occurred over the past 35 years. Seventeen of the eighteen warmest years in recorded history have occurred since 2001, and 2017 was the warmest year on record.

Oceans have absorbed much of the increased heat, with the top 2,300 feet (700 meters) of ocean warming by 0.3°F since 1969.

The Greenland and Antarctic ice sheets have melted greatly over the past thirty years. Further melting of the ice sheets could result in significant rise in sea levels.

The strength and frequency of hurricanes and other extreme storms has risen along with global temperatures.

Series Glossary

atmosphere—an envelope of gases that surrounds the earth (or another planet). Earth's atmosphere, which is composed of mostly nitrogen and oxygen, helps the earth retain heat and reflect ultraviolet radiation.

biodiversity—the variety among and within plant and animal species in a particular environment.

biomass—the total of all living organisms in a given area.

biome—a very large ecological area, with plants and animals that are adapted to the environmental conditions there. Biomes are usually defined by their physical characteristics—such as climate, geology, or vegetation—rather than by the animals that live there.

climate—the long-term average weather pattern in a particular place.

climate change—a change in global or regional climate patterns. This term is generally used to refer to changes that have become apparent since the mid- to late-twentieth century that are attributed in large part to the increased levels of atmospheric carbon dioxide produced by the use of fossil fuels.

ecology—the scientific study of animals and plants in their natural surroundings.

ecosystem—all the living things, from plants and animals to microscopic organisms, that share and interact within a particular area.

food chain—a group of organisms interrelated by the fact that each member of the group feeds upon the one below it.

genus—a group of closely related species.

geodiversity—the variety of earth materials (such as minerals, rocks, or sediments) and processes (such as erosion or volcanic activity) that constitute and shape the Earth.

global warming—a gradual increase in the overall temperature of the earth's atmosphere. It is generally attributed to the greenhouse effect, caused by increased levels of carbon dioxide, chlorofluorocarbons, and other pollutants in the atmosphere.

greenhouse effect—a term used to describe warming of the atmosphere owing to the presence of carbon dioxide and other gases. Without the presence of these gases, heat from the sun would return to space in the form of infrared radiation. Carbon dioxide and other gases absorb some of this radiation and prevent its release, thereby warming the earth.

habitat—the natural home of a particular plant or animal species.

invasive species—a non-native species that, when introduced to an area, is likely to cause economic or environmental damage or harm to human health.

nutrient—chemical elements and compounds that provide organisms with the necessary nourishment.

species—a group of similar animals or plants that can breed together naturally and produce normal offspring.

umbrella species—a species selected for making conservation-related decisions, because protecting these species indirectly protects many other species that make up the ecological community of its habitat.

vegetation—ground cover provided by plants.

watershed—the land where water from rain and melted snow drains downhill into a body of water, such as a river, lake, reservoir, estuary, wetland, sea, or ocean.

Further Reading

Dawson, Ashley. *Extinction: A Radical History*. London: OR Books, 2016.

Finlayson, C. Max, et al., eds. *Wetlands and Human Health*. New York: Springer, 2016.

Joppa, Lucas N., Jonathan E.M. Bailie, and John G. Robinson, eds. *Protected Areas: Are They Safeguarding Biodiversity?* Hoboken, N.J.: John Wiley and Sons, 2016.

Kareiva, Peter, and Michelle Marvier. *Conservation Science: Balancing the Needs of People and Nature*. 2nd ed. New York: W.H. Freeman, 2014.

Kolbert, Elizabeth. *The Sixth Extinction: An Unnatural History*. New York: Henry Holt and Co., 2014.

Lewis, Ewan. *Wetland Ecosystems*. New York: Callisto Reference, 2017.

Mitsch, William J., and James G. Gosselink. *Wetlands*. 5th ed. Hoboken, NJ: John Wiley and Sons, 2015

Taylor, Dorceta E. *The Rise of the American Conservation Movement: Power, Privilege, and Environmental Protection*. Durham, N.C.: Duke University Press, 2016.

Internet Resources

www.worldwildlife.org

The World Wildlife Fund (WWF) was founded in 1961 as an international fundraising organization, which works in collaboration with conservation groups to protect animals and their natural habitats.

www.audubon.org

The National Audubon Society is one of the oldest conservation organizations. It uses science, education, and grassroots advocacy to protect birds and their habitats around the world.

www.iucn.org

The International Union for Conservation of Nature (IUCN) includes both government and non-governmental organizations. It works to provide knowledge and tools so that economic development and nature conservation can take place together.

http://www.nwf.org

The National Wildlife Federation is the largest grassroots conservation organization in the United States, with over 6 million supporters and affiliated organizations in every state.

Publisher's Note: The websites listed on this page were active at the time of publication. The publisher is not responsible for websites that have changed their address or discontinued operation since the date of publication. The publisher reviews and updates the websites each time the book is reprinted.

www.fws.gov

The U.S. Fish and Wildlife Service is a branch of the government that is responsible for enforcing federal wildlife laws, protecting endangered species, and conserving and restoring wildlife habitats within the United States.

www.nmfs.noaa.gov

NOAA Fisheries is responsible for the stewardship of the nation's ocean resources, including the recovery and conservation of protected water habitats to promote healthy ecosystems.

www.nature.org

The Nature Conservancy is a leading conservation organization. It works in more than 70 countries to protect ecologically important lands and waters all over the world.

www.sierraclub.org

Founded by legendary conservationist John Muir in 1892, the Sierra Club is among the largest and most influential environmental organizations in the United States. The organization has protected millions of acres of wilderness, and helped to pass the Clean Air Act, Clean Water Act, and Endangered Species Act.

http://www.greenpeace.org

Greenpeace uses protests and creative communication to expose global environmental problems and promote solutions that are essential to a green and peaceful future.

Index

Numbers in **bold italic** refer to captions.

About the Author

Kimberly Sidabras is a freelance writer and editor. She worked with the World Wildlife Federation for nearly two decades. A graduate of Temple University, she lives near Philadelphia with her husband and three children. She is the author of five volumes in the WORLD'S BIOMES series (Mason Crest, 2019).